THE REAL THOUGHTS OF A SEXUAL SUBMISSIVE

JADE'S DESIRE

Published by Firebrand Publishing Atlanta, GA USA

Firebrand Publishing publishes in a variety of print and electronic formats and by print-on-demand. For more information about Firebrand Publishing products, visit https://firebrandpublishing.com

ISBN: 978-1-941907-19-1 (paperback)

ISBN: 978-1-941907-18-4 (ebook)

Printed in the United States of America

CONTENTS

DEDICATION

Sometimes in life, you come across people that make an impact on your life, and make an everlasting impression on you.

During this thing called life, I have come across different experiences that have led me down different paths in my life. The relationships and sexual paths that I've had and have taken, have led me to an exciting life and a lifetime of sexual desires to be fulfilled.

I can honestly say that these experiences have taught me a lot. They have taught me how to control my body, my sexuality, how to control the man's body, and how to just be in tune sexually.
There are 3 men that I must thank personally for every single sexual experience that I have encountered with them. These

encounters have led me to a deeper understanding of sex, and sex with men.

I want to especially thank the most recent and special person in my life. Not only does he fulfil my sexual desires, he fulfills my needs and wants, and makes me want to be a better me. Who can ask for anything more!

I also want to thank my aunt, for teaching me at a young age the real meaning of sex, and how to please and pleasure a man. Without her, guidance, OR advice I wouldn't be the woman I am today.

I dedicate this book to you.....

Sexually Yours

Jade's Desire

SEX DIARY

Write down your inner most desires, and your innermost dreams.
Write down every sexual thought you have in your head.
Imagine what it would be like, and how it would be.
Now create a scene, and decide what you wanna do first.
Every woman should have a Sex Diary.....

What's your Dream?

ORAL CONVERSATION

Oral Conversation is the best conversation to have.
It's an extremely intimate conversation.
It's a longing feeling, to have him spread your lips apart and suck your clit.
It's a longing feeling of her going down on him, taking him in, licking his base with the tip of her tongue.

Hmmmm...

Using the tip of your tongue, lick his vein, suck his head, and make your lips go pop.
Relax your throat, inhale, take it all in, slob on it, rub it gently, talk to it, become one with it.

Stayed tuned for more Oral Conversation....

A SUBMISSIVE MAN

Men, can you submit to a woman? Can you totally allow a woman to dominate you in bed Sexually? Or do you need to be in control at all times? Are you capable of laying in bed and letting her control you Sexually?

Can she ride you without interruptions? Can she Suck and Fuck you, without you touching her or trying to flip positions? Can you just lay back and Be Completely SUBMISSIVE? Can you let her do what she wants, with No Holds Barred, or are you limited to what she can do and can't Do? How many Men can Submit?

FIRE OR DESIRE

What do you Desire? What sexual desires would you like to fulfill? Ladies, would you like for him to run his tongue down your clit? Fellas, do you want her to just pull your dick out without question and hesitation.

Tell me your Desires, let's talk about them....

FINGER IN MY CLIT...... HOW MANY CAN YOU TAKE?

Oh, I love how he puts his fingers in me, touching me, fingering me, his two fingers, and depending how wet I get, give me three. Put your thumb in my ass, massage my hole, deep penistration, take my clit and rub it rough and soft, 'till I cum, but how many fingers are you putting in me?

Finger fuck me, make me cum, finger fuck me, harder, harder, deeper, I'm about to cum all over your fingers....

TO THREESOME OR NOT TO THREESOME, THAT IS THE QUESTION......

There's a taboo when it comes to a threesome, that it's ok for 2 women to be with 1 man, but it's oh so bad for a woman to be with 2 men. It's gay, or she's a hoe, or a train is being ran on her.

Well dammit, I'm a hoe, and a train is being run on me. The thought of more than one dick, is so fucking fulfilling.... Sucking a dick and getting fucked at the same time, what girl wouldn't want that?

But what's the reason behind the thought that 2 women are ok, and not 2 men? Is that another double standard that we have to deal with? It's sexy for 2 women to be together, and gay for 2 men to be in the bed with each other, afraid their dicks are gonna touch. Well if she has both of them in her mouth, of course their dicks are gonna touch!

What do you think, To Threesome or Not to Threesome, let me hear your thoughts.....

WHAT'S ON THE MENU? WHAT DO YOU TASTE LIKE?

After he is done with the deep penistration, keep it? Can he pull out and you suck his dick to taste your juices? After he is done eating you out can you kiss him and suck his tongue to taste your juices?

How can you expect a man to taste you, and you can't taste yourself? Taste those juices to see how sweet they are, finger yourself and suck your juices off your finger, taste your cum, what does it taste like?

Men, when you cum in her mouth, can you kiss her to taste your cum? After she swallows your cum, cuz spitting is not allowed, after she swallows, can you kiss her? Men, do you have flavor in your cum? What does it taste like? Tell me if you have flavorful cum, and if so, what flavor is it?

THE ART OF MASTURBATION

How do you masturbate? Do you masturbate alone, or with the pleasure of someone watching? Personally I prefer the company of his eyes watching me, him hearing my moans of pleasure, and when I'm done, him watching me taste myself.

Then, him beginning to taste me. I can sit and watch his every stroke, from the base of his dick, to the tip of his dick. Watching pre cum slowly drip out of the head of his dick, makes my mouth water with anticipation. I love to lick it off, take his head in my mouth and suck it out.

I love Sucking out every ounce of cum he has. I love licking his dick from that vein that sticks out when he gets hard. Who better to turn a person on, than the person watching the

pleasures, listening to the moans, and tasting all the juices?
How do you Masturbate?

AROUND THE WORLD IN A DAY

Have you ever been to the Eiffel Tower? If not you should go. There ain't nothing like the Eiffel Tower, a Sit and Spin, and a Japanese Eclipse. How many countries have you been to?

Fellas, would you allow your knees to be put to your chest, and spread your legs apart, and allow your girl to fuck you? Instead of her dropping down and getting her eagle on, would you let her tea bag you in a role reversal?

WATCH ME

Picture me undressing, taking off my bra, caressing my breast slowly and gently, sliding my hands in my panties, and spreading my lips apart. Watch Me.....
Watch Me, finger myself. Listen to my juices as a sound like macaroni and cheese, juices running down my fingers.

Watch Me, as I taste the juice off my fingers, licking them slowly, pulling my nipples, sucking on them. Watch Me, grab your dick and stroke it slow. Watch Me, lick from the base of your dick to the tip of your head

I'm Watching You. Are you Watching Me?....

CAN I SUCK YOU OFF?.....TO DEEP THROAT, OR NOT TO DEEP THROAT

Grabbing the base of your dick, slowly stroking it, and squeezing. As I get to the head of your dick, I move my tongue, up and down, and around your dick, sucking the tip and tasting the pre-cum.

My mouth is watering just the way you like it. Now I'm slobbing, sucking, all the time, watching you and feeling you get hard in my mouth. The harder you get the wetter I get. My intent is to suck you off.

Now I'm Relaxing my throat, getting ready to take you all in. I can feel the tip of your dick, at the back of my throat. I'm squeezing my throat against the tip of your dick, waiting for you to cum down my throat.

I'm Swallowing every ounce of cum you release.

HOW DO YOU WANT IT?....CHOKE ME SPANK ME PULL MY HAIR!!!!

How do I want it? Choke me, spank me, pull my hair.
I don't know how I want it. I don't know if I want it in my ass, pussy, or my mouth.

OOOhhh there are so many holes to choose from! If you put it in my mouth, I can suck on it til it explodes in my mouth, swallow every single ounce.
It's so tasty!

If I put it in my ass, it's so tight and feels so good going in and out. Then you cum in my ass! If I put it in my pussy, I can squeeze my lips around it tightly, I can cum on it, wet it up, bounce on it, and ride it sideways, reverse cowgirl, sideways scissors, so many ways! Fuck it, just put it in me, we can go from hole to hole, what do you think?

FORK UNDER THE TABLE

Take me out to dinner. Take me to a fancy restaurant. Let's sit in a quiet corner so we won't be disturbed. Let's sit side by side so we can be close to each other and feel each other. Let's caress each other, while you finger me under the table. Get me nice and wet. Now my juices are flowing. It sounds so wonderful, and now your fingers are dripping wet! Oops, I dropped my fork. Don't move, I unzip your pants, pull your dick out and slowly suck on it while you squirm and try to focus and not scream.

Scream daddy scream! I wanna hear you say it. OOOOHHH Shit, you mutha fucka, I'ma punch you in yo head, stop. Nope, I'm still suckin, waiting for the explosion, I dropped my fork under the table! I'm looking forward to the dinner we're about to eat, but I wanna swallow you more.

Cum for me under the table, I dropped my fork under the table. Erupt in my mouth, fill me up under the table!

I'll have dessert now, since I dropped my fork under the table.

IS WHAT I'M SAYING TRUE? AM I REALLY WHAT I POST ABOUT?

Yes! The answer is Yes. I'm an extremely sexual person. The thought of having his dick in my mouth, makes my mouth water.

The thoughts of sucking his dick, are like, come on big daddy, bring that dick here, fill my mouth with your thickness, and quench my thirst with your cum.

This one ex-boyfriend told me that I turned him out. He said that he was a square until he met me. Because of the thickness of his dick, no one would have anal sex with him. With me it was, saddle up big daddy! I fucked the shit out of him!

This one guy I was fucking, I was riding him. I closed my legs, and opened his, and put his knees to his chest. I was on my knees as I fucked him, and he didn't know what was happening. I came so hard, that quickly became my favorite position!! Yes, I am what I post about....

SEX EXPLOITS PART TWO

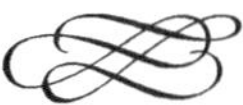

I was with this one dude. He was talking all this shit about what he was going to do. He said he was going to do this and he was going to do that. So, we finally got together and I was waiting for the big bang theory.

Flatline, this dude couldn't lick a fly, or the flytrap it was in. I was bored out of my mind. He was licking all fast and shit, and I'm like, I need you to slow down, because I'm not enjoying what you're doing.

So I stopped him from the torture of him licking me, cuz he definitely wasn't eating me out right. I think he was wanting to rabbit fuck. OMG, fellas, there is nothing fun or sexy about rabbit fucking. I tapped him on his shoulder and asked him why he was going so fast. He said, "I wanna enjoy it".

"Dude, don't you think you would enjoy it more if you slowed down?" I said. I had to lock my legs around his legs just to slow him down, UGH!!!!!

Ok, so next, I tried to give him head, keyword "tried".
This dude was squirming and shit.
"Mutha fucka if you don't stay still," I said.

All I hear is, "damn, if I knew it was like this I would have been here a long time ago."

Needless to say, that sexual exploit never led to another hook up. Rabbit fucking and bad head, a girl can't stand both. I'll give you one or the other, but not both.
What's your sex exploits?

SEX, MAKING LOVE, FUCKIN..... THE ACT IS THE SAME, OR ARE THEY DIFFERENT?

People often confuse the act of sex, making love and fuckin, even though the acts are the same, and the feelings are, similar, they're oh so different.

When you have sex, it's a feeling of a man inserting his dick in you. They say making love is a feeling between the two people that are together, and fucking, oh fucking is on a whole other level.

Making love is supposed to be a passionate act, between two people that are in love. But fucking can be the same. You can be fucking the person you are in love with, even if it's just to shoot one off, and sex is just the act of all three. Which one do you do?

Fucking is that hard pounding, dry my pussy out, get me a rug burn or a war wound, type of sex. It's hard core, heart pounding, sweat dripping, hair nappy, scratches on your back fuckin. Is It The Same Or Is It Different?
You decide.

HOW DARE YOU

How dare you, fuck me like that! How dare you fuck me hard like that. How dare you make me cum so hard! How dare me, how dare you...Suck my dick like that, how dare you swallow my cum like that, how dare you ride me hard and long like that.

How dare you! How dare you eat me out like that! How dare you make me squirt so hard! How dare you let me ride your face like that! How dare you! How dare me, how dare you....Let me fuck you in the ass and cum in your in ass, it's so tight. How dare you! What's your Dare?

ASS IS IN SESSION...HOW TO HAVE PROPER ANAL SEX

Do you know the proper way to engage in, and enjoy anal sex? There are so many women that do not want to have anal sex, because they have the impression that it is going to hurt. Well it doesn't, not if it's done correctly.

So, that's what I'm here for. I'm here to give you instructions on the proper way to have and enjoy anal sex.

When done properly, the shit feels so good, and the orgasm is beautiful.

So, pay attention! There are two ways to have anal sex. Properly, the correct way, and the incorrect way. Let's start with the incorrect way.

Being on all fours in the doggy style position, is not the correct way.

Your body will automatically tense up, which causes pain and discomfort, when attempting anal sex.

The proper way, is either laying on your side, or on your back. You'll already be relaxed, and your body won't tense up. Use the regular missionary position, and instead of him penetrating you from your vaginal area, he'll be entering your anal area. This is much less painful, and also less stressful on the body, and can be enjoyed like regular vaginal sex.

But whatever you do, if you never listen to anything that I say,

YOU ABSOLUTELY NEVER EVER EVER GO FROM ASS TO VAG OR ASS TO MOUTH EVER!!!!!!!!!!

Ass in session.....

CAN YOU RIDE THE RODEO.....THE PERFECT REVERSE COWGIRL

Do you know how to ride a dick without falling off?
How long can you withstand the perfect dick inside you?
How many positions can you use to ride a dick?
Do you know how to do the perfect dick ride?

When doing the perfect reverse cowgirl, there are steps you can take to ensure that the dick is going to stay in the perfect position and doesn't slip out.

Don't spread your legs too far apart, you may get too much air, which causes air bubbles and will make coochie farts.

So, when you climb on top of the dick, keep your back arched to prevent air pockets. With your ass facing his face, keep the arch until you are completely on his dick.

Slide down slowly, and if you can squeeze your lips around his dick, it's truly a wonderful feeling!

Keep your back arched until you're completely on his dick. Raise up midway and allow him to place his thumb in your ass.

While keeping yourself arched over, slowly ride back and forth, grabbing his ankles for momentum and stability.

Don't forget to keep the arch in your back, it allows for deeper penistration and harder climax.

Ride on to Orgasm with the perfect Reverse Cowgirl

FELLAS HEY FELLAS WOO HOO!! PUT YOUR KNEES TO YOUR CHEST

Hey sexy, lay on your back!
Let me ride you. (Like a Harley on a piece of bad road!)
Let me climb on top of you.
Slide your dick in me, I'll close my legs, hold on tight, and squeeze my lips against your dick.
I'll keep you in one spot!

Open your legs and I'll close mine.
Raise your legs high with your feet in the air, and your knees bent.
Pull your knees to your chest, holding them up!
SPREAD THEM LEGS BABY, HOLD THEM UP!
I'll sit up on my knees with your legs up, I'll hold your legs up, grabbing you by your ankles, and I'll fuck you, fuck you with your legs up!

How Long Can You Hold Your Legs Up and Get Fucked?

MOTIVATION

How many rounds can you last? What's your motivation to keep going, giving longer and deeper strokes? How do I motivate you to fuck me the way you do? Motivate me about how hard I'll come on your dick.

Do you think about me slobbering and sucking on your dick? How do you stay so hard, and stay so motivated? Motivation is to keep going, feeling my juices as they completely cover your face and drip from your chin and bottom lip.

Now your beard is soaking wet from my wetness, and all my cum that you released. Motivate me to cum harder! Motivate me to ride you harder!

Motivate me to play unfairly and do all the dirty things you want me to. Keep my face down with my ass up, with a face full of me. Motivate me to squirt!!

How do you stay Motivated!!!

HIM

I can feel him inside of me, his dick inside of me penetrating me so hard and deep. I can feel it, even though he's not around. I can feel his tongue deep inside of me, tasting my soul to its deepest core.

Him....I can feel every ounce of his cum, he enters in me. Every single stroke is like a breath of fresh air going in and out of me.

Him.....knowing that he'll erupt in me with all the passion and desires he has for me, I can see that, just being inside me makes him cum like he's never cum before.

Him....he sucks on my clit and drinks my cum like it's his favorite drink. Swallow my cum baby like you thirst for it, like it's the only taste you want.

Him...waiting for the day that he feels my lips around his dick, just pick the lips you want wrapped around you Him......

~

ORAL SEX...SUCKING DICK....GIVING HEAD...THE DIFFERENCE BETWEEN THE TWO.....

Do you suck dick, or do you give head? There is a difference, and if you don't know the difference or don't know there is a difference, you shouldn't have his dick in your mouth.

Some women think, sucking dick is just having the dick in your mouth, playing with it, to either get it hard, or just to get the whole thing over with.

Well lady, put the dick down and step away from it. You don't need to have it in you, in your hand or in your mouth.

That's dick abuse!

Giving head, I love giving head. It's the act of making love to his dick, stroking it, slobbing on it, caressing it, getting to know and allowing it to get to know you.

Giving head is so sensuous. It's a slow stroke of the tongue and hand, and at the same time, it gives you control of his dick.

What's the easiest way?

It's the easiest way to swallow him whole and touch the back of your throat, but that's another story. You don't have to open wide, the gentle touch is going to get you where you need to be.

Slide your hand up and down his dick.
Lick the pre cum, lick his vein that pops out, suck the tip of his dick ever so gently.

Make sure your mouth is watery, not too much, but just enough for him to know what's coming next.

Position yourself in a way that's comfortable for you to perform. Yes, you are performing. You are performing the art of giving head.

Grab it gently, suck the tip, lick the pre cum, lick his vein, take him in slowly, moan, perform slow strokes up and down his dick.

Stroke his dick with your hand. Give a gentle twist to his dick and put it in your mouth at the same time.

Watch him squirm. Slowly relax your throat to take him in and suck him whole.

And that is the difference between sucking dick and giving head....

IMAGINATION...HOW DEEP IS YOURS

Ladies, close your eyes, imagine his touch, imagine his smell, imagine how he feels. Can you picture it?
Now use your imagination to feel him inside of you.
Use your imagination to feel you sliding down on him.
How does it feel?

Fellas, imagine how she feels. Imagine her taste, lick your lips and feel her clit. Suck her pearl and play with it, until it tightens up and releases the warmth that she is holding for you.

Now ladies, imagine his dick, growing harder with the thought of you. Imagine him going inside of you, deeper and deeper, now you're waiting for his eruption inside of you. Can you feel it? Can you touch it? Can you taste it, and can you imagine it?

~

TO TOYS OR NOT TO TOYS, THAT IS THE QUESTION....

Men, how comfortable are you with having toys in the bedroom? Can you handle a dildo as an extra enhancement? The dildo, let's just say the enhanced dick may be bigger than yours.

Are you intimidated? Can you still perform? I want you to watch me while I take it. Watch me as I put it in me, in and out, deeper and deeper, making me, cum on it, and suckin' on it the same way, I suck on you. Can you handle Toys in the bed?

Maybe I'll put the Ben Wa balls in me, and push them out, so that you can watch my muscle control, and see how my clit and pearl tongue beams at the mere thought of you!

Can you handle toys in the bed? Maybe I'll cum harder. Maybe you're asking yourself, "Is she cuming from the dildo, or from the thought of me watching her fuck herself?" If you know me, then you already know the answer!

Let's play with toys in the bed, so you can watch me cum.
Let's play with toys, so you can see how my muscles release with passion!

So, I'll ask you again, To Toys or Not To Toys? Can You Handle It?

SLIDE SOME OIL TO ME

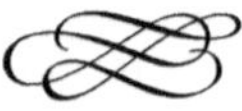

As I'm laying down caressing my breast, I'm sliding my hands down my cleavage, grabbing my breast, sucking my nipples, licking my areola, playing with my clit, and feeling all of my wetness drip down my fingers. I'm tasting my juices.

They taste so sweet, mmmmmm... I wish he was here to slide me some oil. She sounds like juicy heaven, slipping through the gates of orgasmic destiny, with a touch of summer mist dew.

Slide Some Oil To Me. I'm moving my fingers in and out, listening to my juices. They sound so good, because I'm getting wetter and wetter, with every stroke. Let's add another finger, and let's add a toy!

Slide Some Oil To Me. I stick my finger in my ass, and still have my fingers in me. I alternate, dildo, finger, dildo, finger. I can't decide which one, is best but they both feel good. Slide Some Oil To Me.....

BOND...BUT NOT JAMES BOND

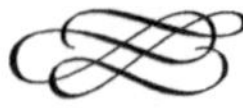

Blind fold me, tie me up, with my arms above my head. Bend me over with the perfect arch in my back. Smack my ass daddy, smack it hard, let me hear it! Tie me up, so that I can't move. Tie me up so that I won't move.
Hold me down daddy, spread my legs apart and strap them down so that they can't move, keep them still don't let them move.

Bondage is a perfect way to Bond Keep me close daddy, take control of me. Have me the way you want me. Tie me up, and put yo dick in my ass, smack my ass, choke me, daddy! Spread eagle me! Spread my ass apart, spread my clit, suck my pearl, and do all the little naughty things you wanna do. In Bondage do what you want to do! Bond, But Not James Bond!
Are you into Bondage?

DAYDREAMING....IS IT FAKE OR IS IT REALITY

Lay me down with my eyes closed. Imagine me on top of you, grinding, rubbing, pumping, feeling, sucking, and tasting. I've never been tasted like this before.
I've never been sucked like this before. I've never had my clit licked, my pearl, or my peach, oh, so many names for it. But whatever you wanna call it, it's never been eaten like this before.

Am I dreaming or is this reality? Is it a fantasy, is it a desire, or is this something that I really want to happen.
Oh my God, it feels so good, it feels so real. I can't believe this is happening. I can't believe I'm enjoying this so much. Oh my God, I've never cum like this before, my legs are shaking so bad.

Am I dreaming, can this be real? Tell me that I'm dreaming. Is this something that I really want to happen? No it can't be, no it shouldn't be, no I can't.
Oooops sorry, it was a dream. But do you know what or who I was dreaming about?

HAVE YOU EVER

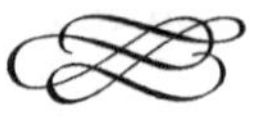

Have you ever fucked someone that you knew you weren't supposed to? You'd be fuckin, and knowing that you were great? You fucked him so good you had to pat yourself on the back? You swore you would never fuck him again, but that dick was so good you couldn't help yourself. He sucked your clit and used the two finger method.

If you have to ask or wonder what the two finger method is, then you don't need to be on this chapter, that's oral sex 101. Back to the story. I came ready. I showed up with nothing but thigh high boots, a bow tie, and a trench coat, knowing what I wanted and what I was gonna do.

Not only did I not take my coat off and fuck him, I sat him on the chair, tied his arms behind his back, pulled his pants down to his knees, sat on him and fucked him well. I came, I sucked, and I conquered!

HAVE YOU EVER…SECRETS

I know you can feel me looking at you. I know you can feel me staring at you, undressing you with my eyes, and secretly on my knees sucking you off, while you scream my name.

Can you keep a secret? If I fuck you the way you wanna get fucked, can you keep it to yourself? When you walk past me, can you not look at me, knowing that we just fucked?

My secret is, I wanna fuck you. I wanna sit next to you and get wet just looking at you. I want to think about all the dirty things we did, and dirty things I wanna do.

Can you keep a secret? I wanna feel you inside me, pulsating, with deep pounding thrusts. I crave deep strokes, the kind that make me grab the headboard, making sure you pound my guts harder and harder!

You are my best kept secret. Can you keep a secret?

MY CLIT

My pearl tongue is perfect. It's a pretty little peach. She can speak to you and say hello, she can squeeze your head, like we're shaking hands, like she's saying, "Nice to meet you."

She smiles with a glistening sparkle. The mere thought of you brings tears to her eyes. She tightens up when she smells you, she throbs when she hears your voice, she sings when she knows you are near. Boi oh Boi, when you touch her, she erupts and she overflows, like the river running deeper and faster than you can ever swim in.

When she screams, she lets out a yell so loud, and releases the warmth that gushes all over you. She showers you with joy.
Have you met her?
My Clit....

SHE IS SO WET

OMG, I'm walking around work today, and thought about him. I got so fuckin wet, that I felt the juices at the mere thought of him.

Shit, she was dripping like crazy.

I felt like everybody at work knew I was thinking about him. I just knew everybody saw that I was horny, almost as though I had a bulls-eye on my forehead!

My mouth watered, as I thought about giving him head.

My mouth watered just thinking about his dick, and how I not only wanted it in me, but in my mouth, sucking every ounce of his cum out of it.

Geesh, this man drives me crazy! The mere thought of him makes me horny as fuck, and wet as shit.

Does Your She Get Wet.....

SOMETIMES I

Sometimes I sit and wonder to myself, damn, where did all of this come from, and why am I so open with sex? Why do I need to push the limits?
Like damn, why do I have to convince someone to have and enjoy anal sex the way I do? I feel like damn, do you really know what you are missing, with not having a dick in your ass?
Like damn, why are you just sucking his dick instead of making love to it? Then you wonder why he has a side chick?
Sometimes, I wanna be like other women, and just be like fuck it. I'm not doing that, or eww that's not lady like, but fuck it. The sight of his dick changes all of those crazy ass thoughts and personal restrictions.
Like you see this dick, are you crazy? How can you not try a dick in your ass, or swallow cum? Shit if anything, you'd be

better off swallowing, for a healthy looking skin tone. It keeps you looking young, keeps the crows feet away.

I'm me. I'm comfortable with who I am, and the skin I'm in. It's not me it's you.

Suck a dick and get nothing, give head and get everything...

Sometimes I......wonder.

SOUNDS JUICY TASTE JUICIER......

That sound is like music to his ears. She's so wet and juicy, and she tastes even sweeter!
She sounds like stirring macaroni and cheese. The cream is thick and tantalizing. She will definitely leave you wanting more!

When she cums, it's an eruption like you've never seen before. It's hot and thick and will leave you dripping wet!She's juicy like a peach, and as sweet as a plum.
She never leaves you unfulfilled, or never unsatisfied.

She's always thirst quenching. She tastes sweet and not over filling, cuz you'll definitely want more. She is juicy and tastes sweet.

LADIES LET'S TALK

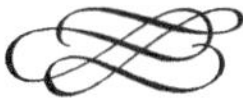

Ladies, stop giving him bad sex. Stop asking for him to fuck you hard, and eat you out, but you just give him the basics.

Stop being basic and be a beast. Give head, swallow, let him put his dick in yo ass, and try different positions. Stop being a one position trick! Get on top and ride his dick 'till you're numb and he's sore. Start out slowly, lean forward, and put the perfect arch in your back. Grab his ankles, give a good slow grind.

Pick up the speed, when you hear him moan, and when you feel him moving around. When you get that first smack on the ass, you know you're doing it right!
When he smacks you on the ass, you know that dick is getting

hard. Now the question is, how are you gone fuck it, or waste it?

A waste of good dick, doesn't just happen. Make sure you squeeze them lips around his dick, and push down for deep penistration, squeezing your lips around his dick. Stop wasting dick, fuck the dick right. It's a crime against dick to have dick abuse. Stop abusing the dick. Lick it, suck it, and fuck it!

SQUIRT

I love how it feels when I cum, especially when I cum in his mouth. He takes his fingers and tongue and slurps it all out, using the two finger method. There we go with the two finger method again. I can squirt all day from his fingers and his touch. I love cumming on his dick, but squirting is my favorite, the best!

Now, let me explain the two finger method, in a short version. But I'd rather talk about squirting, and how different it feels to squirt, versus how it feels, when I cum.

Squirting is like a release, a powerful thrust that comes through my cooch. It's so different, it's like turning on the water hose and releasing the pressure. It's different when I cum. When I cum, a feeling of warm gooey goodness, that slides down his dick. When I cum, it also releases pressure, but in a different way. Its' thick and creamy with a joyful delight.

Trust me, not every woman can squirt. It's definitely a gift. Also, not all men can make a woman squirt, he definitely has to be tongue gifted. Now which one would you prefer, Squirt or Cum?

POSITIONS

THE DIFFERENCE BETWEEN THE TWO....MISSIONARY OR SEXPERIMENTAL

Are you boring in bed? Are you a missionary one position type female? Are you the type that will ride only if you have to, type of female, then sit on his dick for two minutes, and then make him get on top?

Well, that's truly a complete waste of dick riding and time. When he wants you to ride him, he wants to feel you deep inside, and look at you, and enjoy the site of you being on top of him. He wants to caress your breast, hold your hips, and look at you, while he enjoys watching your eyes roll in the back of your head. Sit on top of his dick.

Bend over and kiss him, Suck his nipples, fall back with the arch in your back, and grab his ankles so he can penetrate you deeper. Let him feel your muscles tighten, waiting for you to cum. He wants to feel your juices run down his dick. He wants to feel your muscles contract and squeeze the tip of his head, while you are on top.

You are in control of his every move. Hold his hands down, don't let him move, make him become submissive. You control every action being on top. Then watch him cum, watch his toes curl, watch him hold his yell in to keep from screaming.

After he cums, when you get off his dick, watch him squirm, and shake, and as you walk away and look back, ask him, "You Ok?"

The Difference in Missionary and Sexperimental.

CAN YOU FEEL IT

I can feel you even when you are not around. My lips throb at the thought of you, the sound of your voice makes me wet, your touch, your taste, makes me scream.

I can feel you tasting me, going inside of me, knowing that when you erupt, I'll take in every ounce of your cum.

I can taste you. I can taste the sweetness of your cum as it slides down my throat, and I swallow. Can you feel me cum on your dick? Can you feel that powerful thrust that cums when you hit the spot, when my lips squeeze your dick?

Can you feel it? Can you Feel me caressing your dick with every muscle I have, as I slide down on you? Take me in, suck me, lick me, taste me, Feel Me.

TWO FINGER METHOD

Fellas, I know I have mentioned this before, but now it's time to discuss and give a tutorial about the Two Finger Method.

If you're not doing the two finger method when you are giving her head, you are doing it wrong. Fellas, here's the thing. When you're going down on your girl, you have to know she is welcoming you, waiting for you, so you feel the anticipation of her wetness.

Spread her lips apart with your fingers not your hand. Take your thumb and finger and open her up. It's like saying hello for the very first time, so take your time.
Once you have her lips spread apart, place your finger on her clit and move it back and forth, not too hard, but not too soft

either. You want her to feel everything you are doing, you're fingering her and giving her head at the sametime.

As you suck her clit, take your tongue and motion it up and down as you keep your finger in her, and massage her clit. The two finger method is the best way to fulfill and bring a female to orgasm, and make her wet and cum all over you.

IT FEELS SO GOOD

I stand in front of him, take his shirt off, unzip his pants, guide him to the bed, and proceed to lay him down
He smiles like he's never been touched before. He has been but never has he been touched like this before.
*I climb on top of him and proceed to give him head. I kiss him, caress him, and show him how I feel. His moans of passion tell me he loves what I'm doing. His yell tells me I'm sucking the right spot. I love to hear '**Got Damn**' when I give him head, and leave him speechless.*

I also love when he's standing up, and I just put his dick in my mouth and he's yet again rendered speechless and weak. It feels so good to finally have the One, to have Him, and know at the end of the day He is the one! Finally it feels good.

BEND ME OVER

I want him to bend me over and fuck me. I want him to take me by the hair and fuck me. Bend me over while I suck on your finger, fuck me. Take your dick and put it in me, let me cum on your dick.

Fuck me from behind, bite my neck, pull my hair, put the arch in my back, and show me just how much you want me. Take me from behind.
Pound me, fuck me, hold me, take me, give me the penistration that I desire. Cum in me. Cum for me daddy!

Show me from behind how much you want me. Spread my ass cheeks apart, put your finger in my ass, make me cum and squirt all over you. Will you bend me over?

~

I LIKE IT I REALLY REALLY LIKE IT....

I really like how you spread my legs apart. I really like how you put your tongue on my clit. I really like how you suck my pearl tongue. I really like how you feel when you go inside of me, I really like how you it hurts so good.

I really like how deep you go inside of me. I really like how I feel when I cum on your dick. I really like the way you slide inside of me, caress my breast, and the gentle touch of your kiss. I really like how I scream your name when I cum.

I really like how you say, "Baby Oh shit!" when you cum. I really like it, Do You?

HE LOVES ME

He loves the way I lick his sack. He loves how I take my hand and stroke his dick, ever so gently, or roughly. He loves the way I taste his pre cum. He loves the way I lick his vein when it pops out, and the way I suck the tip of his dick.

He loves how I wrap my lips around his dick, but which lips does he love the most? Coochie lips, or mouth lips, they both make him cum. He loves how I welcome him into me, and how I make him feel like a sweet morning misty dew, with sprinkles of lavender.

He loves how I cum down his dick, and cum for him so hard that he feels my lips pulsate on his dick. He loves how I suck his cum out, and swallow every ounce of his sweet sweet cum. He loves how...

I CAN FEEL IT

I can still feel you inside of me, the way you tasted me, the way you suck on my breast, ever so rough, but gently. I can still feel the way you made me cum on your fingers, while you pleasured me with your touch. But oh boy, what I can definitely feel was you sucking my clit, and making me squirt, and cum when you used your tongue!

I hope I didn't drown you! You know how much I love squirting, and how much I love to squirt in your mouth with such powerful thrust. And the cum that came, is the calm before the storm. I can still feel how you entered me with that dick of yours, and how you fucked me like you haven't fucked in so long. Fuck me, suck me, play with my clit, boy did you do it all! I can still feel it, can you?

HALLS...MINTS...ICE...WHICH ONE

There have been so many ideas, and ways people share, of what feels good while giving head. Which do you prefer? Do you enjoy the added incentives in sex, while giving head?

Some people say that the heat from a Halls gives you pleasure. There are certain Mints that give off different types of heat. It is a hot and cold sensation. Then there's using Ice. It's definitely not like the other two, but why do so many people enjoy using Ice during sex?
During sex, for the female, it's the sensation of the clit. When you put ice on her clit, she swells up for excitement and pleasure, boy does she swell up!

So how about taking an ice cube, and a Halls, and putting it in your mouth at the same time, and watching her swell and get wet? Now, when you give him head with Ice and Halls in your mouth, and he feels the actual hot and cold on his dick, while you're licking his head, with the ice cube on the tip of his dick, while you're going down on him quickly and coming back up...that will make him scream!

Having the cold on his dick while sucking it with the heat from the Halls, will make his dick hard as a rock and cum like a river. Now which one do you choose, Ice, Halls, Mint.....

HE SAID

"I want you to fuck me," he said. "I want you to cum down on my dick, and lick every ounce off."

"I want you to suck me so hard, that when I cum, I cum more than I've ever cum before." He said, "My strokes are harder when I fuck you. I cum harder when I fuck you," he said.

He said ,"I need to feel you, I need you to cum down my dick. I get so hard just thinking about you when you're not around. My dick gets so hard just looking at you, feeling how wet you are, while you squeeze your lips around my dick, while I lay on my back and caress your breast.

Let me suck on your nipples and smack your ass, let me put my finger in your ass and feel how tight your ass is, and how wet you get." He said, "Let me spread your ass cheeks open and go deep in yo ass, let me cum in yo ass it feels so tight." He said, "Just let me cum wherever you want me to cum!"

YOUR RELATIONSHIP......

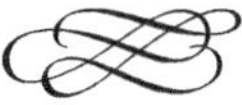

How is your relationship? Can you define the difference between your relationship, and how the real world sees your relationship? Do you know the quality of your status, and how your spouse and or significant other sees you?

How secure are you, to hear the truth of what he or she thinks of you? Can you handle how he really sees you? Men, can you handle the truth of how she really sees you? Do you know how you think you are seen, is not how you are really seen?

Take the time to ask her how she sees you. Ladies, take the time to ask him how he sees you. Once you see how each of you is seen in each other's eyes, you can now ask if you like what you see, and if you're willing, or wanting to change their view of how he or she sees you. Your Relationship.....

BEEN HOLDING BACK

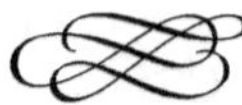

He's so mad, because I haven't completely given myself to him,
He like, "What the fuck you holding back for?
Why the fuck you holding back?" "You mad? lol.

Oh my sweet baby, the joy that she brings you is everlasting, the cooch that you feel is wet and juicy." The cum you feel is hot, warm and good to the touch and taste. It's sweet and is still fulfilling."

I still will make you scream my name, I have an everlasting effect on your dick, just like your dick has an everlasting effect on me. You want me to give you everything? You want my whole book, you want me to sit and spin, you want me to reverse cowgirl, you want the horse in the pie hole?

I'll give in to every desire and wish you want, but please, once I stop holding back and give you everything, be careful what you wish for. The lips, both sets, the tongue and the throat, is a dangerous place to be! Sorry, I'm not holding back anymore.

IT'S SO TASTY TOO

Oh I love this man so much, when he cums in me, it's like the eruption of lava exploding everywhere! I look forward to catching, wherever he wants to put it.
It's just me, that wants to catch it in my mouth.
It drives him crazy that I want him to pull out so I can suck it out.

I'm like, "damn, can I have some?" His cum is so sweet, I love how it feels going down my throat, how it's warm and hot, and feels good sliding down my throat.

With something so sweet, you don't spit it out. That would be a waste. Do you spit out candy? Do you spit out your food? No you don't, so why would you spit him out?

Oh the taste of him! I look forward to seeing his vein pop out, and when his head tightens up, and he gets harder than a light pole, I just know that his sweet juice is about to erupt! Let me catch it... It's So Tasty Too

HE JUS WANNA

He jus wanna taste me, he jus wanna taste my juices, didn't I give you enough, geesh aren't you full yet Man!

He jus want me on top of him, riding him, straddling his dick, sliding up and down, and listening to my juices going in and out. He jus wanna taste his fingers after he fingers me, and hear me moan with pleasure, and feel my juices run down his fingers.

He jus wanna be like, "Damn girl, you mine and all mine! This feels so good, and I love being in you!" He jus wanna say cum for daddy, cum for daddy on this dick, let me feel them lips around my dick.

He jus wanna feel me give him head, and lick his vein and suck on his head, and let all that cum slide down my throat. He jus wanna....Would you let Him?

TONGUE KISS ME

I want him to kiss me. He better spread my lips apart and play with my tongue, tongue kiss me, slowly take his tongue in and out, and suck on my tongue.

Tongue Kiss Me, take my pearl and open it wide. Watch it glisten and listen to her speak. She will smile and talk to you. Just kiss her right, and she will sing a song and cry for you all at once.

Tongue Kiss Me, show her the depth that you are willing to go and how hard you're willing to go for her, to make her feel it inside. Tongue Kiss Me from the back. Pound it in 'till she cries a river for you, and she screams with excitement! Will you Tongue Kiss Me...

FINGER...TONGUE

Will he let me play with his ass? Will he let me put proper placement in his ass? I welcome him in my ass will he welcome me in his ass?Will he allow me to place a finger or a tongue? I take my tongue and play with his ass, to watch him cum, while I jag him off and play with his ass.

If I take my finger and play with his ass, will he squirm and wiggle so I can't get a hold on to that ass literally? I want my finger in his ass. I want the cum that he is going to erupt so I can taste and swallow. I want him to watch me while I give him head and play with his ass.

I want to see him cum, I want to hear him scream. So the real question is Finger or Tongue.....

YOU BETTER

Boy when I see you, you better Fuck me so hard, that I run dry. No one has ever dried me out, will you be the first? You better take these lips and suck them like you sucking the meat off a chicken bone, while my cum is the grease that is around your mouth, glistening like a shining star!

Boy I'm telling you, that You better bend me over, smack my ass so I can hear it, and leave a hand print!

You Better make me squirt and cum at the same time.
Let me ride you long and hard, so you can feel me run down your dick, while my lips are wrapped around your dick.
You Better.....

HOW DO YOU SUBMIT

Are you willing to let go and allow your spouse to control you sexually? Are you willing to sexually obey his or her every command? Are you willing to lay down with no questions asked, spread your legs apart, and let me tie them to the bed? Will you let me tie your arms to the headboard? Are you willing to submit?

Turn on your back, toot your ass in the air. Don't move, let me take my whip and whip you, since you've been a bad boy/girl. Let me spank you til you learn your lesson!

Bend over and spread eagle, close your eyes and repeat. I'm a bad girl/boy and I want to be punished, I want to feel how deep you can go in me. Punish me!

Pour hot wax on my body and lick it off. Teach me how to be a good girl/boy, but I promise I'll be a bad girl/boy just so you can punish me over and over again.

Take your tongue and give me 12 lashes to my entire body. Know that once you're inside of me, or I'm on top of you, those lashes are gonna hurt so good.
Now, the question is Do You Submit...

SLIPPERY WHEN WET

The mere thought of his dick turns me on. I can taste his cum, it's so sweet, the tip of his dick fits in my mouth perfectly. I get so wet just thinking about his dick being in me, sweet goodness. I think about him, and start throbbing like crazy.

How in the entire fuck can the thought of someone get me so wet? She is slippery when she is wet, gotta keep wiping her off. Slippery when wet, is so dangerous.
It's dangerously wet, the taste, and the touch of her is dangerous when she is this wet.

She's uncontrollable, intense, and unpredictable. She will have you going crazy! Slippery when wet is fun, but will have you doing shit you never thought you would. Slippery when wet, will have you smiling all the time, paranoid, and wondering all the time.

Can you handle her when she is slippery when wet……

HE SAID

He told me that I turned him out. He said that I was the first person to introduce him to anal sex. He said, he had never cum from oral sex before me, and that he was feeling some type of way because of it.

He said, fucking me is bad for his health. He said that I make a nigga wanna stalk me, keep me in the house.
He said, I did things to him that he could only wish for, or think about in his dreams. The touch, the taste...

He said that the way that I touch him, makes him feel like no other man should. The way I stroke his dick is the touch of magic, and he can cum on my hand and watch me lick it off.
These are all the things that He said.....

MY VIRGINITY......DOUBLE PERSONALITY

You wouldn't believe who took my virginity, and who turned me into helping me create my alter ego. Lol, my cousin. He was so gentle with his touch, he taught me the true meaning of what sex is, and how to embrace my touch, and my feelings.

He taught me how to please a man with every move I make, every stroke I give, and how he is touched. I created an alter ego. She does things that I wouldn't.

She is Jade, she is the sexual ego that goes where men don't think they want someone to go. Jade makes men give into their inner desires, and fears. She has a way to convince you that you belong to her, and only her. Jade is dangerous. She was created when I lost my virginity, she is my double personality.
Do you want to meet her.....

FUCKING HIM

I'm fucking him for a pass time, just to have something to do 'til it's time for it to come to an end. Fucking him is fun. Playing the role is even better. Fucking him is climatic it's like riding a bike and cumming every time I pedal.

Fucking him brings me a sense of control that I have over him, he allows me to do whatever I want to him. Fucking him is definitely not boring, the way his dick gets hard makes me wetter than I can even imagine. The way he puts his tongue in me and sucks on my clit, is so fulfilling, he makes me cum every single time he sucks my clit.

Fucking him is fun....

MASTURBATING

He makes me want to masturbate. He makes me want to take my fingers and fuck myself for pleasure and fun. He makes me wanna bend myself over and fuck myself in the ass, smack it. Oh the way he makes me feel and how he looks at me! The way he looks at me makes me wanna cum all over myself, my cum can fill up a cup and run it over with his looks.

I can sit in front of him and masturbate and squirt all over him, just by him watching me. He makes it easy to orgasm. Masturbating to the sound of his voice is so soothing. If he knew I wanted to just masturbate in front of him would he like me.

Would he let me masturbate and cum standing over him so it will run down my leg as he licks it off? Would he let me masturbate and squirt all over him while he drinks my squirt, or will it be too much for him to handle?

Can I masturbate in front of you and not fuck you, or would you want to fuck me after I masturbated in front of you, as you watched me cum. Will you masturbate for me......

DAYDREAMING

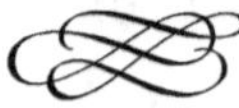

Shit, here I go again. Laying here thinking about how I want his dick in every hole that I have. I'm day dreaming about cuming on his dick and sucking it off, and taking in every ounce of cum he gives me.

Damn, why does this shit keep happening, why does this dude make me so fucking weak? Why in the entire fuck do I dream about waking up, fucking him, and sucking him off? Why do I get so wet just at the mere sound of his voice?

I'm day dreaming about having his dick so hard that it won't go down, and he fucks me as long as I stay wet. Just fuck me, don't stop just fuck me! Daydreaming, sometimes I wish it was a real dream.....

THIS DUDE

This dude is so fucking sexy, the sex appeal that exudes him is fucking intoxicating. His swagger is off the chain, the way he looks, the way he speaks, is like damn... I'm wet as fuck!

When he touches me I'm ready to cum all over the place.
My panties be so fuckin' wet, I'm sure glad I started wearing panties again, or I'd be fucked up! He makes me cum from every way he touches my clit. Shit, when he fingers me, when he tastes me, and mutha-fucka especially when he fucks me.

This dude is fuckin' reckless. There's a lifetime of things that I would, could, and can do to him, just to make sure that those fingers, tongue, and dick touches no one else.
This dude, Shit, that's all I can really say. He fuckin leaves me speechless, and extremely dehydrated.

HIS QUICKIE IS LIKE

Quickies are supposed to be a fuck just to hold you over, you're not supposed to cum from a quickie. When a quickie is like a great fuck, and leaves you weak with bruises, that's the best quickie you can ever have.

His quickie is like OMG!!!! I got bruises on my leg. I'm still trying to figure out why my forehead is sore, I'm glad I don't have a bruise. His quickie made me cum like we were having a great sex session.

His quickie had me bent over trying not to squirt all over the place. His quickie, shit, is all I can say. His quickies are fucking dangerous...

LADIES DO YOU

How do you release your passion screams? Do you bite your lip to contain your screams, do you let it out, or does it depend on who you are with? For those of us that are in relationships, does it depend on where you are?

Ladies, do you allow yourself to be sexually free, or do you contain yourself? To be a lady it or they say that a lady shouldn't do that. Ladies, do you still hold back sexually and not allow yourself to enjoy the greatest feeling in the world?

Ladies, do you just lay there, just to get it over with, and fake an orgasm because he doesn't or just can't find or hit that spot? Does this make you wanna just get it over with? Well, there is a solution for that problem.

Know your body, teach him how to fuck you, teach him where your pleasure spots are, teach how to make you cum.

But ladies, if you don't know your body, you can't teach him your body.

I LIKE IT

I like it when he bends me over and fucks the shit out of me, and ask's me do I like how daddy fuckin' me. I like it when he gives me head and finger fucks me at the same time. It builds up my cum, and how I'm gonna cum, and sometimes he makes me cum and squirt at the same time. That's a true gift

I like it when he lays down and allows me to fuck him, not knowing how I want to fuck him, no questions asked. He might be nervous, cuz he doesn't know what I'm going to do. I like how he moans while I'm giving him head, and talks shit while I'm licking him, and showing him just how I feel about him.

I like how I cum while he's still fuckin' me.

He pulls out and goes back in me while I'm cumin, oh my goodness it feels so good to have that feeling, it makes me cum more. I like it, well damn I just like him.

MY DESIRE

My desire is to have his dick in me as much as I can. Just to feel him deep inside of me, grabbing me and stroking me. My desire is to sit on his face and cum down his throat, and he swallows every ounce of my cum, the same way I swallow his cum.

My desire, shit, I have so many when it cums to him. I just can't count them all. Will he fulfill my desire or will it just be a quiet desire?

Will he desire my every need, will he desire to keep that rock hard dick, That mutha fucka is beautiful when it's hard. Geesh, ok I'm back. My desire, damn, I wish he was here to suck on my desire......

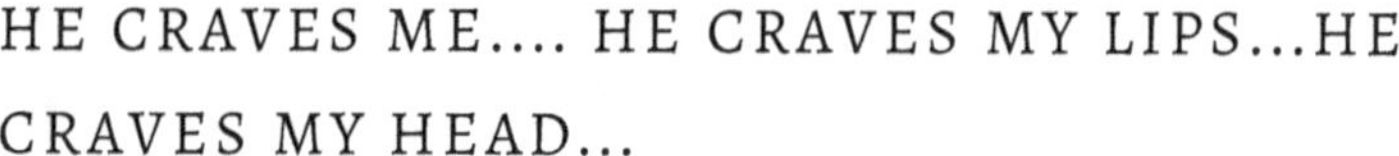

HE CRAVES ME.... HE CRAVES MY LIPS...HE CRAVES MY HEAD...

I love the way he craves me. It drives me crazy, it turns me on in a way that I've never been turned on. I get so wet that I can't wait for his dick to be in me. The way he looks at me drives me crazy. The mere sound of his voice gets me so fuckin' wet, that it is sick.

He loves kissing me. The way my lips feel against his dick is the perfect feeling. The way his tongue feels on mine is soft and juicy. I look forward to every single minute that we're together. The touch of his dick, the taste of his dick, the thought of his dick, is a feeling that I can't explain.

He looks forward to having his dick in my mouth, and cumin in my mouth, and watching me swallow gets him even harder. So what is a girl to do, but to start all over again! If he craved you, the way he craves me, what would you do?

LIVING LIFE

So, a few years back I met this guy. I think it was about 1999. I was at this club with the girls, and as usual like all females that go out, I had on a really short skirt, and some cute sandals and my toes were out.

So, he watched me the whole night, without saying a word. My girl asked me if I was going to say something to him, staring at me all night. At first, I was like what? T hen I realized that not only was he looking at me, he was looking at my feet. I didn't pay it any attention because hey, I did have on sandals, and it was February so I guess I would probably have done the same thing. But he eventually said something to me, and told me that I had the prettiest toes he had ever seen, and he is not a foot person.

So, after that night, we talked and started dating. Boy did we fuck. His dick was thick and juicy, and he had the perfect size and girth. Even though he was a little older than I was, sexually, I had an advantage. There were a lot of things that I was into that he wasn't, but there were also things I convinced him into doing.

He says it to this day, that I'm the only person that can handle him sexually, that he had anal sex with, and that ever made him cum, giving him head. Trust me, I feel the same way. Sex just wasn't the same after him, so now I'm just... Living my Life. How about you?

TEA BAGS HONEY AND CREAM

Ladies, what do you think about tea bags? Do you like it or dislike it? Do you feel some type of way, when a guy wants to tea bag you?

Do you even know what tea bagging is, and how to do it, and where the concept came from? Hmmm, let's see how we can have the conversation about tea bags, honey, and cream.

He stands over me with my face under his ass.
I open my mouth and await his balls to enter my mouth, then he drops down, and bounces up and down, like a tea bag. Now, if you are any good, you should be able to tea bag and jag him off at the same time and You get (him?) excited and he cums. That's where the honey and cream comes in, but you gotta

know how to do it. It's the male version of men dropping down and getting his eagle on, while she sucks on his balls and jags him off. So ladies, let's tea bag our man, and get the honey and cream!

DOES YOUR JAW GET TIRED

How long can you suck his dick before you begin to complain that your jaw is tired, or is getting sore and tired? What's the longest time you can give head, and suck him off before you start complaining about how long it's gonna take him to cum?

Well damn, here's my take on it. If you're gonna suck his dick, suck it, and get on top of it, and try to cum or make him cum. Or, give him head and keep giving him head until he explodes in your mouth. Don't complain about it, just do it.

Giving head gives you all the benefits, that sucking dick don't. Now the thing is, there is no such thing as complaining, he may not be a two-minute brother when it comes to getting head. He may not know how to cum when getting head. He's probably never experienced that feeling before, so be patient.

If your jaw starts to hurt, then you are not holding your mouth properly, nor do you have your body in the correct position. So, practice always makes perfect, cuz like I've said a thousand times, anybody can suck a dick, it takes love and passion to give head.

It takes knowledge to know how to sit and position yourself, or to lay, so that your jaw won't hurt. So, now the question again is.....Does your jaw get tired?

SAME SEX

Well ladies, when did you have your first same sex experience? Did you enjoy it, or did make you know that a dick is what you need in your life?

Well, let me tell you about my first experience with the same sex. It was a totally scary and exciting experience, all at the same time. One of my favorite aunts, the one who made me the sexual deviant that I am today, helped me with my experience. I tried it, but I was too afraid to enjoy it, in fear of being labeled or thinking that I was something that I didn't want to be.

Well, I tried it a second time. I relaxed and went all the way, well, not completely all of the way. I couldn't eat another woman's cooch, yeah sorry couldn't do it, but I did allow her to do me. Well it's safe to say that I'm not into women, and I know that I want a dick in me at all times. I do not want to bump uglies with another woman.

But I will say that I believe that at a certain age, I do believe that women should at least try it with an open mind, experience it. Now, I will tell you that the oral sex that comes from a woman is impressive, but I'd rather it come from a man. So, have you ever had your dose of same sex yet?

HIS TONGUE

His tongue feels like silk on my clit, his tongue feels like cotton on my ass, as he spreads my lips apart and sucks my clit. He takes his fingers and spreads my lips apart and sucks like there is no tomorrow.

Geesh, I wish I could sit on his face forever. I wish his tongue was attached to my clit. His tongue is simply magical. Seeing as though the tongue is the strongest muscle in the body, and brings the best pleasure, it makes me scream and moan.

His tongue, ooh my goodness his tongue! What more can I say about his tongue? I wish I could share his tongue, but I'm selfish and somebody might want to keep his tongue for themselves.

So nope, I'm keeping that tongue all to myself. It's a great feeling when the tongue and dick is that good.
His tongue...damn, that's really all I can say

I LIKE MY BOOTY RUBBED

I don't know why I love getting my booty rubbed when I'm laying down, but it definitely puts me right to sleep.

Maybe it's the feel of his hands running across my body, or the thought and anticipation of me wanting to have anal sex. But the fact of the matter is, that I enjoy my booty being rubbed while I'm going to sleep or just laying down.

When he rubs my booty, I really want him to take his finger and run it up the crack of my ass.

Please put your finger in my ass, please rub my booty, smack my ass and squeeze it real hard. Bite my booty, nibble on my booty, leave just a little bruise.
Rub my booty......

SEX IS IT MENTAL OR PHYSICAL

When you have sex, are you mentally connected or are you physically connected? When he gives me head, I wanna look down on him as he sucks on my clit. I wanna see the look in his eyes when I cum and listen to him slurp all my juices.

I want all eyes on me, while I'm stroking every inch of his dick, with my hand, then watch him squirm while I massage every inch of his balls with the other hand. He needs to watch me lick and suck his pre cum as it leaks.
I wanna hear him moan with pleasure and see the sexual lust in his eyes, and how much he wants his dick in my mouth.

Is the connection mental or just physical? When you're making eye contact during oral sex and even sex, it's the connection that is made Nothing turns me on more than being watched while I'm in between his legs or laying him on his back.

I want a mental connection while I watch him and while he watches me. Sex is more than physical, it's all mental. Without that connection you just fuckin' for nothing.
That orgasm will be weak without the connection, but when that sexual connection is made that mutha-fuckin' orgasm is soo off the chain So make a connection and cum like a mutha-fucka......

SPIT OR SWALLOW.... IS THIS REALLY A SERIOUS QUESTION

Girl, why are you not swallowing? Now don't get me wrong, you can't suck everybody's dick, and you definitely can't swallow everybody's cum.

Now the reason I encourage swallowing of the cum, is because it's the bond between you and your spouse, fuck buddy, side piece, whatever you wanna call them.
But like I said you're not supposed to suck everybody's dick, and please don't swallow everybody's cum. There are some men who have funky cum, yeah that shit is nasty and it leaves a bitter after taste, and geesh it makes you belch like a mutha-fucka.

So please by all means swallow cum. It makes for a protein shake, you need your daily dose of protein, it keeps for a young looking skin, and a good healthy living. It also keeps side bitches away. They say side bitches do what the main chick won't do, so if you're not suckin' and swallowing, I say you better get to suckin' and swallowing.

And don't ever spit, it's a waste and extremely disrespectful, not only to the dick, but also to the art of giving head, and reaching the ultimate goal. The Cum.....

DICK AND COCK...WHY DO BLACK MEN HAVE A DICK AND WHITE MEN HAVE A COCK....

Why is there a different name for something that we women love to have in every hole that we have?

Black men have dicks and white men have cocks. Please somebody tell me why it's a difference. It does the exact same thing, so why do we call it something different, because it looks different?

It tastes the same, it's not less filling, it fills the same hole that a black dick does, it fucks the same, sometimes it even fucks better. The length comes in different sizes just like a dick. It cums just like a dick, it smacks your ass just like a dick.

Some of them are nastier than a dick. We also have to remember that it was the cock that invented, eating coochie. They are the masters of that shit, so why don't white men have a dick? Please explain to me the difference between a dick and cock....

HEAD

All he wants me to do is give him head, all he wants is to feel my lips wrapped around his dick.
He wants to feel my hands jagging him off, stroking him while I lick his pre cum off his dick.

He says just put the tip in, meaning just put the tip of his dick in my mouth, knowing good and damn well I oh so enjoy giving him head.

So, I played the three little pigs on that dick. I sucked and I sucked 'till all the cum came out. Even though this one particular time I didn't swallow, doesn't mean that I don't swallow. It means he had me in an awkward position and I damn near choked, lol!

But the next time I have that dick in my mouth and that cum flows out, I'm drinking it like milk. Since he's always drinking cranberry juice as he says, but it's not, so let's see what that cum tastes like. Head.......How do you enjoy it?

KISS ME THERE

Kiss me here, Kiss me there, Kiss me everywhere. I wanna feel your lips on every part of my body. I want your lips to caress me, suck my nipples, taste my clit, just kiss me here, kiss me there, kiss me everywhere!

Kiss me where it counts, kiss me so that I can show you how much I enjoy you kissing me.

His lips are like soft gentle pedals with a rough edge.
He spreads me wide, and tastes me deep, and sucks my hole..
Swallow my juices, make me whole, touch the inner me, kiss me where it counts.

HIS VOICE...HER VOICE

Ladies, do you hear his voice? Does it make you wanna scream and cum all over yourself? Fellas do you hear her voice and get so hard, it's like a brick? Well, I do. The sound of his voice drives me fuckin crazy. It's so fuckin sexy, and I know along with that sexy ass voice, comes that sexy ass body and that dick, geesh that dick.
Ok, back to the subject at hand. I can sit and listen to him just ramble off and not say shit, it's just his voice that does it to me.

I close my eyes and picture him between my legs giving me that fuckin head! Oh good golly miss molly, that head, Shit.. See how I get off topic when I talk about him, that is fuckin crazy. The swagger he has, comes through the phone. He listens to every word that I say, pays attention to what I say! That makes me even wetter!

A mutha fucka that has swagger that comes through the phone, is a dangerous mutha fucka. His tongue is lethal in every way.

The pressure of his tongue does so many things in so many ways. It releases the stress that I hold in my vagina, and he licks all that stress away. His tongue is lethal when I need him to be a sounding board, and just tell me what to do instead of asking. Just let that tongue unleash, tell me what to do!

Now, what does her tongue do? Does her tongue drive you crazy when she wraps it around your dick? Does it drive you crazy when she's just kissing you, knowing that she is going to put her lips around your dick? Does her voice say, "Put that dick in my mouth," every single time she answers the phone? Does it say, "Cum for me daddy?"

Can you just sit and look at her mouth and get hard, knowing that she is going to devour your dick in her mouth? You can rest assured that whichever way it goes, we have that one person that we hear on the phone or in public that turns us on in some form of way! His Voice....Her Voice

SIDEPIECE

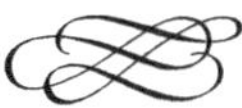

I was his side piece, but he wanted me to be his main piece. I forgot I was a side piece, gave that dude a head piece.That's what the fuck I get for swallowing that piece. Damn, look at what the fuck I got myself into, now he won't leave me alone, and tries to keep me from being with anybody else.

Dude, I know my role in the piece, do you know your role in this piece? My peace is to be yo side piece 'til I want peace.

I'll fuck you how you want me to fuck you, but when I'm tired of fuckin you, oh I'm gonna fuck somebody else. Know your role. You're my side piece, and I'm your side piece. So be at peace with what you have.

AIN'T NUTHIN BUT A 'G' THANG BABY...

Ladies, have you ever sat back and thought about the men in your life, and what they do and don't do? Well I gotta 'G' that's good. Lawd, he makes my clit cry, makes my toes curl, and makes me cream like there is no fuckin' tomorrow.

Sliding down his dick is like the perfect mix of lavender and weed, it fits perfectly and makes me cum and squirt at the same time. I've never had someone make me do both, and damn, 'this dude', yeah, I've mentioned him before, Shit, cuz he does it for me.

Shit, there's really only one other man in my life that has ever made me feel like this, had the full package. Damn that's scary! I've had a very interesting sex sexperimental life.

Now I can add him to it, the way he looks, the way he touches me, the way he just carries himself. Shit ladies, if you don't have a 'G' in your life you'd better get one. And 'G' ain't No Gangster.......

A NATURAL WOMAN

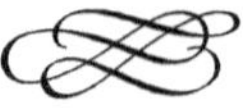

Ladies, let's talk again. This man has me so confused and fucked up in my thoughts right now it's scary! The mere thought of this man, sends my mind racing, and puts a smile on my face. Geesh, it's like he takes away everything that's bothering me without saying a word. He just puts it straight and to the point, no sugar coating. He handles me like no other man can, and he can just look at me and I know that everything is going to be ok.

When I have a stressful day at work, he understands and listens to what I have to say. No matter how many questions I ask him, even if he doesn't want to answer them, he does. He's a straight shooter, and he scares the absolute shit outta me. Our conversation is so much fun and silly as shit, and gets better and better all the time. We can just sit and talk for hours, no sex, and it's the best conversation I've ever had.

He looks at me like no one or nothing else matters, especially at that moment. As soon I see him looking at me like that, he looks away and smiles. That smile can stop a speeding train. He makes me feel like he understands me, and that's scary. He makes me feel like a Natural Woman......

HIS DICK

Ladies, have you ever had a man or been in a relationship with a man, whose dick was so perfect, that nothing can keep you from it? Is his dick so perfect that the mere thought of it makes you wet as fuck? Does it make your mouth water and cream just a little bit thinking about it?

Well ladies, I have one. If I can wake up to this dick everyday, there would never be a dull moment. Not only is his dick good and fulfilling, he is my friend, and he's turning into my best friend, which is the best thing a girl could ever ask for. The person that fucks you like no other, takes his time and doesn't rush. He sucks on my nipples like I've never had my nipples sucked before.

He caresses my body. His touch is gentle, his lips are perfect, his tongue is magical and does all sorts of special things. Sometimes they are not even sexual.

But his dick is just so deliciously tasty, juicy, soft, and that vein! His cum, it's all perfect to taste and touch. If you don't have one, you'd better get one, cuz. His Dick.....

WE DID A THREESOME

Well well well.....Here we go with this topic, threesomes. I've asked this question before. Are you into threesomes?

I had a couple of threesomes, more than I actually wanna admit. I've done a threesome primarily with two men, but I've also had a threesome with another woman and a man. But there's something about two men at the same time, it's intoxicating.

Maybe it's my desire to be greedy, especially if it's good. Knowing that I can be open with the person that I'm with and not worry about sneaking around But sometimes I wonder if he is really ok with doing a threesome, or if he is just doing it because I enjoy it.

He can not handle the thought of me being with another man, yeah he don't like that shit at all, so what is a girl supposed to do? Sexually he is very satisfying, but I enjoy being with more than one man. He gives me the sexual pleasure that I need, and he fulfills my every desire, all the way around.

He fulfills my mental, my physical, and my sexual desires, and makes my heart skip a beat. So why oh why do I enjoy two men at the same time? Maybe it's a mask to keep me protected, to keep my heart covered, or maybe one man just is not who I'm built for. We did a threesome.....

WHAT THE ENTIRE FUCK

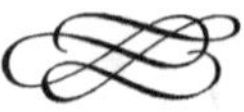

What the fuck have I gotten myself into? Geesh I can't stay out of trouble. I can move to a whole other state, and still find myself figuring out how the fuck I got myself into it.

So here's the pickle, my sex life has always been exciting, it has never been boring, I have tried several things in my life, sexually. Some I like, and some I'm like, why the fuck did I just do that? Then there are the yes mutha-fucka let's do this shit again!

This is the nastiest shit I've ever done and I wanna keep doing it. Give me some more dammit, give me some more! I get myself into more situations that I can ever imagine, and I try to figure out how and why. But damn the shit be so good that I can't stop! What the entire fuck......

PHONE SEX

Phone sex is for the mind. If you can make love to my mind, or even fuck my mind, you are definitely talented. Being able to mind fuck someone is definitely hard to do. You have to be able to visualize with your words. I close my eyes and see you doing all those things you want to do to me.

You need to be able to make me wet with your words, make me cum with your words, and penistrate me mentally instead of physically. You most certainly can make me cum with your dick, but can you make me cum with your mind, and your words? Your words are sexual, your words are powerful, your words are dirty, nasty and sexy. Your words and your voice put together, can make me cum. Phone Sex.....what can you say to make me cum from my mind.

WHEN HE LOVES YOU BUT CAN'T TRULY LOVE YOU......

How do you win the heart of someone that loves you, but can't love you the way he wants to? His heart is divided in two parts, where he is, and where his heart is. How can a person make a decision on the truth of the heart?
Will he make a decision with his heart, and choose his heart and not his comfort? Why do situations like these come up? How do you prevent getting your heart broken, when you know it's going to happen?
Is there a way to prevent a broken heart? Can you, at all times, protect your heart? True heartache is the worst thing, and the hardest thing to get over.
Al Green said it best, 'How Do You Mend A Broken Heart." Is there really a way to mend it, especially when you know where his heart is? But some people choose comfort over love.
When He Loves You But Can't Truly Love You...

HE MAKES MY KNEES WEAK

I get weak just thinking about him. Knowing that I'm going to see him, makes me cream like crazy. His voice, his eyes, his everything is the perfect mix of the perfect thug, professional, hood, classy, suave qualities.
You name it, he has it all.

All my life I created a man that didn't exist, just so I wouldn't get my heart broken. But ladies I'm here to tell you there is nothing that you can do, to protect your heart.

His sex is so fucking good, and his head is fucking off the chain. I've said this before and I'll say it again, he is the only man that has ever made me cum and squirt at the same time. Shit, there goes the neighborhood! He handles me like no other man can or has been able to handle me. It's hard to handle me, and he does it with ease, and the shit is such a fuckin turn on.

It's crazy that I get excited when he puts me in my place, and it's like "Yes Daddy!" lol. Then it's like, "Did this mutha-fucka just talk to me like that?" But I'm turned on and pissed off at the same time. Who does that? I do, that's who. He Makes Me Weak...

GARGLE.....SWISH....NO SPIT

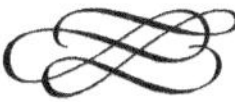

I've never gargled on his dick, and I've been wanting to for a long time now. Do I think he can handle me gargling on his dick? I don't know. Can he handle the back of my throat tickling the tip of his dick, just getting him more and more aroused?

How fast will he cum if I gargle on his dick? Will he pop like a weasel, or will he be able to contain his cum? I can't wait to have him feel the back of my throat, and hear it sing a song for him.

I can't wait to have him hear my yodel on the tip of his dick, swish it around in my mouth, and gargle like it's mouthwash. But I just don't spit it out, spitting is a complete no-no. Gargle....Swish....No Spit....

HE FINALLY GOT IT.....I FINALLY DID IT

Since the first time we met and starting fucking around, and the first time I gave him head, he has been wanting to cum in my mouth.

I enjoy a good nut in the mouth as much as the next girl (or maybe not), but I feel like that's an extremely intimate part of sex. Like I've said once before, "You can't swallow everybody's cum."

So, I finally decided against everything in me, to start letting my guard down with him. I don't know why, but I am, and I am setting myself up for failure and a broken heart, and it's fucked up and I know it.

Well I wanted to give him head, and I wanted to swallow his cum, so I did. I licked, I sucked it, and low and behold I swallowed. I think it was good, but I was disappointed because I was expecting a lot more cum.

I think he was disappointed because I was disappointed. I was just hoping and anticipating that the build up would have given me more.

At least I can say, I Finally Did It & He Finally Got It.

SEX PLEASURES...

My sexual desires of men intrigue me everyday. Knowing how sexual I am, the extreme desires that some women feel, make them feel as though they shouldn't do it.
The pleasures of sex are the desires of the soul. Opening the body to various tricks of sex, can lead to sexual desires being fulfilled. I love having his dick inside of me, the feel of it, the taste of it, the round of it.

So sit back and enjoy the ride, thoughts, and sexual desires Of A Sexual Submissive.

Stay Tuned.......

WHO IS THE SEXUAL SUBMISSIVE

I grew up in a family of open sexual conversation. I was taught at an early age about sex, the do's, the don'ts, the how to how not to, the good, the bad, and the ugly of sex and relationships.

Sex was and still is a open forum discussion. Just because I talk about sex, doesn't mean I wanna fuck you. It means that sex is my favorite topic.

Do I do everything I talk about?

Oh Absolutely!

My aunt taught me the ways around a dildo at a very young age. She taught me how to perform oral sex and when not to suck a dick. You can't suck everybody's dick, they're not worthy, and it's just pure nasty to taste a million dicks.

Same sex experiences have also shown me that I definitely love the feel, touch and taste of a man, but I'm very comfortable around situations where most people are uncomfortable.

I've done threesomes and all. I'm very open sexually, and I'm willing to try something at least once, ok I'm lying. I'll say I'm willing to try twice, depending on what it is. I might have to try it again, just to see if I really like it or not.

Join me on my Podcast, to listen and have discussions about these and other everyday topics on:

- blogtalkradio.com/thesexualsubmissive
- Instagram @sexualsubmissive1
- Facebook AnnetonetteConner

www.ingramcontent.com/pod-product-compliance
Lightning Source LLC
Chambersburg PA
CBHW071019180726
48291CB00004B/1543

* 9 7 8 1 9 4 1 9 0 7 1 9 1 *